Judo

Paul Mason

W
FRANKLIN WATTS
LONDON • SYDNEY

First published in 2007 by
Franklin Watts
338 Euston Road
London NW1 3BH

Franklin Watts Australia
Level 17/207 Kent Street
Sydney NSW 2000

© Franklin Watts 2007
Series editor: Jeremy Smith
Art director: Jonathan Hair

**Series designed and created for
Franklin Watts by Painted Fish Ltd.**
Designer: Rita Storey
Editor: Nicola Edwards
Photography: Tudor Photography,
  Banbury

A CIP catalogue record
for this book is available
from the British Library.

Dewey classification: 796.815'2
ISBN: 978 0 7496 7409 0
Printed in China

Franklin Watts is a division of Hachette
Children's Books, an Hachette Livre UK
company.

Note: At the time of going to press, the statistics
and player profiles in this book were up to date.
However, due to some players' active participation
in the sport, it is possible that some of these may
now be out of date.

Picture credits
Peter Tarry/Action Plus p.21; Bob
Willingham pp. 7, 14, 17 and 26.

Cover images: Tudor Photography,
Banbury.

All photos posed by models.
Thanks to Anjola Daniel, Steve De-Meis,
Jack Eaglestone, Thea Hawlin, Arthur King,
Adam Wittiner, Emily J. M. Wittiner,

Japanese words, which are common in
judo, are shown in italics, *like this*.

All the techniques in this book are
described as though being done by a right-
sided judo fighter.

Taking part in sport
is a fun way to get fit, but
like any form of physical
exercise it has an element of
risk, particularly if you are unfit,
overweight or suffer from any
medical conditions. It is advisable
to consult a healthcare
professional before beginning
any programme
of exercise.

Contents

What is Judo?

Judo is a way of defending yourself. It is also an Olympic sport. From its beginnings in Japan, judo has become popular all round the world. Today there are judo fighters of all ages and almost every nationality.

The Birth of Judo

Judo was first invented in 1882. It was invented by a Japanese man called Jigoro Kano. At the time, a fighting style called ju-jitsu was popular in Japan. Kano used some of the techniques of *ju-jitsu* to invent judo.

Judo Contests

In a judo contest, or bout, two fighters face each other. Each tries to throw the other to the ground. Fighters win points for making a throw. The better the throw, the more points it wins. Sometimes one throw is so good that it wins the contest outright!

The fighters sometimes end up carrying on the contest lying on the ground. They can win points for holding their opponent down. This is called groundwork.

A class for young judo fighters, who are called *judoka*. They listen carefully to the advice of their instructor.

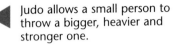

Judo allows a small person to throw a bigger, heavier and stronger one.

You can find out more about the different judo scores on page 26. The referee decides the scores. He or she is on the mat with the fighters, making sure they obey judo's rules.

Judo first appeared at the Olympic Games in 1964, though only men were allowed to take part. Women had to wait until 1988 before they could compete in Olympic judo contests.

There are other judo contests for all grades of fighter. They include small contests between local clubs, regional and national championships, and international competitions like the World Championships.

Judo for Self-Defence

Judo fighters use their opponent's aggression to defeat them. This makes it possible for a smaller person to win against a bigger one. Because of this, judo has become very popular for self-defence.

Respect and Discipline

People in judo are expected to show others the proper respect. Everyone – practice partners, teachers, referees and judges – must be polite and respectful to each other. Discipline is also important. Students are expected to listen carefully to their instructor, and try as hard as possible to follow his or her advice. In judo, the referee's decision is final. The fighters must accept it even if they do not agree with it.

Jigoro Kano, the inventor of judo (on the right), teaching a student his techniques. Because judo began in Japan, many of its special words are Japanese.

A Tough Test

In 1886, just four years after judo had been invented, the new sport faced a tough test. The Tokyo police held a contest between judo and *ju-jitsu* fighters. There were 15 fights. The judo fighters drew two - and won the other 13! Jigoro Kano's new sport was a big success.

Judo Basics

The only gear you really need to start learning judo is the special clothes that all judo players wear. Your judo club will provide the rest of the equipment for learning.

Judo Clothing

Judo clothing is very simple. It is made up of a white jacket and trousers, and a special long belt. Together, these are called *gi*. The jacket and trousers must be well made, so that they do not rip during practice. *Judoka* fight in bare feet, and do not wear jewellery. If you have long hair, it is best to tie it up in a ponytail during practice. In contests, one of the fighters wears a blue *gi*, so that the judges can tell the two fighters apart.

Reinforced collar for strength.

Long sleeves can be gripped by opponent.

Tough stitching does not rip when pulled.

Belt.

Loose trousers, above ankle height.

Judo Schools

Judo schools are called *dojo*. Some are permanent, but most share their space with other activities. This means that all the equipment must be packed away after each class.

The Practice Mat

The main piece of equipment for a judo school is the soft practice mat. This is called the *tatami*. The *tatami* stops fighters from hurting themselves in a fall. It also provides the area in which fighters must stay during a contest.

Practice mats can be any size, but contest *tatami* measure 8 metres square or more, with a 1-metre danger area (warning the judoka they are close to the edge of the contest area) and a 3-metre safety area (where the padding continues in case anyone is thrown out of the contest area) on the outside.

This young *judoka* is ready for action!

How to Tie a Judo Belt

1 *Place the very middle of the belt on your stomach.*

2 *Loop each end behind you and bring them both back to in-front.*

3 *Cross the right end over the left end, then thread it up behind both loops.*

4 *Cross the left end over the right end, then tie them tightly together. Both ends should be equal length. If they aren't (see opposite), your teacher might tell you to tie the belt again!*

A well-tied belt, with a tight knot and both ends the same length.

Watch out!
Always knot your judo belt at the front, or you could hurt your back by falling on the knot.

Judo Grades

Older *judoka* have a system of ten grades to show how good they are. These grades are called *kyu*. A fighter who reaches the tenth *kyu* is allowed to wear a black belt.

Junior *judoka* have different grade systems depending on which country they come from. Usually there are 18 grades, called *mon*. Every fourth *mon* has a new belt colour. The order of the colours from beginner to expert is:

- white
- yellow
- orange
- green
- blue
- brown

To progress through the grades, fighters have to show senior judges that they have learned the rules and techniques of judo well.

Training

Learning judo is great fun, but it is also hard work! Even getting ready for the class takes careful preparation. It is worthwhile, though, because proper preparation helps judoka to avoid injury.

Warming Up

Warming up is stretching your muscles and doing gentle exercise, so that your muscles are relaxed. It is important to get your body ready for a judo class by warming up. This is because things happen fast in judo! One minute you will be standing opposite an opponent. The next you might be twisting around to throw them, or lying in a heap on the practice mat!

Judo Muscles

These are the main muscle groups *judoka* use:

- Shoulders
- Neck and upper back
- Chest
- Stomach muscles
- Arms and legs

It is important that all of these get a chance to warm up before you take part in judo practice. Judo teachers will always make sure that their students are warmed up before the lesson begins.

The Thigh Stretch
Lift one leg up behind you. Hold your foot, then gently pull it towards your bottom.

Stretching

The Shoulder Stretch
Reach your arms up above your head. Stretch them backwards, feeling the effect on the muscles under your upper arms and in your shoulders.

Stretching

◀ **Side Stretches**
With your feet shoulder-width apart, put your right hand on your hip or leg. Lift your left arm up, then bend to the right.

Neck Rolls
Tip your head sideways, then roll it down so that your chin is on your chest, then back up the other side. ▶

Remember to Breathe
When doing stretches, take deep breaths to help you relax your muscles. If you hold your breath, the stretches will not work as well.

Building Strength

Judo uses an opponent's attacking power to defeat them. Even so, having strength in the muscle areas listed on page 10 is important. *Judoka* aim to build up their strength without overdeveloping their muscles, as this would make it harder for them to move quickly.

Young *judoka* should not use weight training to build their strength. Instead, they can use 'resistance training'. This involves exercises such as push-ups, sit-ups and pull-ups. It is important not to do too much of this type of training when young, though. The best training for judo is judo practice!

Building Speed

The best *judoka* are able to react very quickly when they see a chance to defeat their opponent. But how do they build this skill? The answer is, by practising hard!

Top-flight *judoka* practise the same technique day after day, month after month, year after year. They repeat it thousands of times. In the end, they are able to do it without thinking. In a contest, their body is able to react as soon as the moment is right.

Falling

When people start learning judo, most are hoping to be taught how to do spectacular throws. In fact, the first thing new **judoka** learn is how to fall over. Sounds easy – but it isn't!

Breakfalls

Judo falling techniques are called breakfalls. The Japanese word for them is *ukemi*.

The most essential techniques for *ukemi* are:
1) Keep your head tucked in and your back bent forwards. Your neck and back are much less likely to be hurt in this position.
2) Use your hands, feet, arms or legs to spread the force of the fall. Falling on only one part of your body is likely to injure you. There are special *ukemi* depending on whether you are falling forwards, backwards or sideways.

Your head and neck should not touch the mat in this rolling breakfall. Instead, the fall is broken as you roll from one shoulder, across your back, and to the opposite hip.

▼

A Forwards Breakfall Roll

1 The palms of your hands should be flat on the floor. Tuck your chin in against your chest.

2 With a bent-forwards back, roll forward on to your right shoulder. Your left leg comes up and through the air first.

Play it Safe
Tuck your head into the safest position by looking at the knot of your belt.

12

Protecting Yourself

Learning to fall properly is important for safety reasons. Just crashing into the mat any-old-how would be very dangerous. It could easily lead to a bad injury.

Knowing that you are able to fall safely is also good for your confidence. It allows you to feel braver when practising new techniques. If they go wrong and you are thrown, you are much less likely to get hurt if you have learned how to fall safely.

In this backwards breakfall, the *judoka* has used her arms and hands to cushion the force of the fall.

It is important to keep your chin tucked in.

A Backwards Breakfall

Falling in Competition

Falling well is also an advantage in competitions. If you fall badly, for example flat on your back, your opponent scores lots of points. If you fall well – onto your elbows or hands, for example – your opponent wins fewer points.

3 *As you roll over, slap the floor with your left hand and arm. This will absorb some of the force of the fall. You may be able to carry on the roll and stand up – ready to start fighting again!*

First Skills

Once they have learned how to fall, new judoka *learn the basics of attack and defence. These need to be learned well – they are as important to the very best* judoka *as to the newest beginner.*

Judo Postures

A posture is a way of standing. In judo, there are different ways of standing depending on whether you are attacking or defending:

• Natural – standing upright with your feet up to shoulder-width apart, but no further.

• Left and right natural – the natural posture, but with either your right or left foot forward.

• Defensive – this is similar to natural posture, but with your feet more than shoulder-width apart and your knees more bent.

• Left and right defensive – defensive posture, but with your right or left leg forwards.

Standing in these postures helps *judoka* to keep their own balance while trying to catch their opponent off balance.

Craig Fallon

Date of birth: December 18, 1982

Nationality: British

Contest record:

2006 European Championships: Gold

2005 World Championships: Gold

2004 Prague A Tournament: Gold

2003 World Championships: Silver

2003 Rome 'A' Tournament: Gold

2003 Paris Super 'A' Tournament: Gold

2003 European Championships: Silver

2002 Commonwealth Games: Gold

Craig Fallon (shown here in blue) is a great all-round fighter, famous for using his flexibility to twist out of opponents' attacks, however strong their grip.

Taking Hold

To throw your opponent in judo, you need to have a good grip on them. The skill of taking a strong hold of your opponent is called *kumikata*.

There are many different ways to take hold of your opponent. Top *judoka* practise their throws and other skills starting from all sorts of different holds. One of the most common is shown in the photographs.

1 *Grip on to your opponent's collar with your right hand. Next get a good grip on the bottom of their left sleeve, under the elbow.*

2 *From position 1, pull on your opponent's sleeve. Get your right arm under their armpit, and grip on to their belt.*

Getting a good grip on your opponent can make the difference between throwing them in the contest or not.

Attacking Weaknesses

A key principle of judo is that you should use your opponents' weaknesses to defeat them. Top-level *judoka* are good at quickly finding out what their opponents are not good at, then attacking them there.

Breaking Balance

Once you have a good grip on your opponent, it is time to start looking for ways to throw them. The way to do this is to catch them off-balance. Breaking an opponent's balance is called kuzushi.

Attack and Defence

An opponent standing in one of the basic postures (see page 14) usually has good balance. But in judo, you can't both just stand there in a basic posture – you must try to win the contest! In competition, if the judges think a *judoka* is not attacking enough, they will give points to the opponent.

Opponents are most likely to be off balance while attacking you, or when defending against your attack. They could be off balance because they are coming towards you, in which case you may be able to use their movement to pull them forwards into a throw. Or they could be backing away, which might mean you can trip them so that they go over backwards.

Breaking an opponent's balance and throwing them using an inner reaping throw.

First the attacker (in blue) breaks the defender's balance backwards and to the right.

Next, he sweeps the defender's left leg out to the left. With his balance already broken, the defender cannot stop the throw.

Leverage Points

Leverage points are places that help a push or pull to move an object. For example, when you open a door, there are two leverage points. The first is the door hinge, which holds one edge of the door still. The second is the handle – pushing or pulling on the handle makes the door move.

Judoka aim to create leverage points on their opponents. Once they sense that an opponent is off balance, they push or pull in the same direction. So, if the opponent is going backwards, they push backwards too.

But this is just one leverage point. A successful throw needs two! To create this second leverage point, the *judoka* might put his or her leg behind the leg of the opponent. Now, the opponent's feet are like the hinge – motionless, while the opponent's body is like the door – about to slam!

Kosei Inoue

Date of birth: May 15, 1978

Nationality: Japanese

Contest record:

- All-Japan champion 2001, 2002, 2003
- Asian Games champion 1998, 2002
- World champion 1999, 2001, 2003
- Olympic champion 2000

Kosei Inoue is one of only four *judoka* who have managed to win three world championships. Famous for his all-out attacks, Inoue was often able to win his contests with a single throw.

Kosei Inoue throws Nicolas Gill of Canada in the 2000 Olympics judo final. This is the throw that won Inoue the gold medal. The photo shows how a successful *judoka* uses leverage points – in this case, the leg, arm and shoulder – to throw an off-balance opponent.

Hip Throws

*Many judo throws are based on a type of throw called a hip throw. The very first judo throws included the hip throws, and they are still an important part of every **judoka's** attacking technique today.*

Timing and Leg Strength

In hip throws, attackers use timing, plus the strength in their hips and legs, to throw their opponent. Using the power of your legs to lift your opponent over your hip is a key skill in this throw. Your arms are used only to lock your opponent into position for the throw. *Judoka* who simply try to pull their opponent over will find hip throws very tricky.

The Large Hip Throw

Many judo throws are based on the large hip throw, which in Japanese is called *ogoshi*.

The Large Hip Throw

1 As you step in to attack, change your grip so that you have a hold of your opponent's belt.

2 Step in to attack, turning your body so that your back is to your opponent. As your hip pushes against the opponent, use your grips on their sleeve and belt to lock them into place. Bending your knees will help you get into the right position.

3 Straighten your legs, and lift the opponent over your hip. If you have timed your attack well, they will continue forwards and tumble to the mat.

The Floating Hip Throw

1 *Turn into the attack, putting your right foot just inside the opponent's right foot. Your feet will be quite far apart at this point.*

2 *Quickly bring your left foot in towards your right foot. This will tip your weight to your left, and lift your opponent up onto your hip.*

3 *Turn your hips to the left and throw the opponent to the mat.*

The Floating Hip Throw

In Japanese, the floating hip throw is called *uki goshi*. This was one of the very first judo throws. In fact, it was one of the techniques taught by the inventor of judo, Jigoro Kano (see page 5).

The floating hip throw is different from the large hip throw because the attacker does not bend his or her legs. Instead, the power for the throw comes from the turning speed of the attacker.

Timing and Practice
All throws work best if they are performed quickly and with good timing. To get them right, they must be practised thousands of times.

Shoulder Throws

Shoulder throws are even more spectacular than hip throws. The opponent is thrown right over the attacker's shoulder, meaning they can be thrown high in the air before crashing back to the mat. In competitions, successful shoulder throws often win the bout. Of course, to take your opponent by surprise with such a big throw takes great speed, and a lot of training!

Shoulder Throw Basics

All shoulder throws have some things in common:

• The attacker has to get low down to be able to throw the opponent over their shoulder. Bending your legs helps to do this.
• The attacker's changes in body position and grip on the opponent set the throw up, putting the opponent in the right position for the throw to happen.
• The power for shoulder throws comes from the attacker straightening their legs, once the opponent is in the right position.

The Two-handed Shoulder Throw

1 *Face your opponent with your feet shoulder-width apart and your right foot slightly forwards. Grip their collar with your right hand and their sleeve with your left. Pull on your opponent's sleeve, turning your hand so that your thumb twists down.*

2 *Keeping a grip on the opponent's collar, turn and slide your elbow through so that it is tucked under their armpit. At this point you will be facing away from your opponent with their chest locked against your back. Bring your left foot in and carry on turning to your left to lift them off the ground.*

Ryoko Tamura

Date of birth: June 9, 1975

Nationality: Japanese

Contest record:

- Asian Games champion 1994
- World Champion 1993, 1995, 1997, 1999, 2001, 2003
- Olympic Champion 2000, 2004
- Silver medalist, 1992 and 1996 Olympics

She is only 1.46 metres tall and weighs less than 48 kg – but Ryoko Tamura is a giant of the judo world. Holder of the world title for an amazing 10 years, she is so popular in Japan that a character in a cartoon strip, 'Yawara', is based on her!

3 *Pull with your left and right hands to keep the opponent moving over your shoulder. Straighten your legs as you pull and twist: your opponent will be thrown over your shoulder.*

This photo of a *judoka* performing a two-handed shoulder throw (called *morote seoi nage* in Japanese) shows why it is important to learn your breakfalls well!

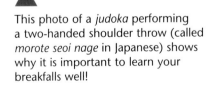

Reaping Throws

Reaping throws sweep an opponent off their feet. There are several different kinds of reaping throw. *Judoka* can sweep an opponent's feet away using their legs, feet – or sometimes even their hands!

Inner and Outer Reaps

When describing a reaping throw, coaches talk about 'inner' and 'outer' reaps. In inner reaps, the attacker sweeps away the opponent's feet from between their legs. The attacker puts their foot or leg between the opponent's, and sweeps it out to the side.

In an outer reap, the attacker starts the reap from outside the opponent's legs, then sweeps inwards and back, instead of out and away.

Reaps Using the Hips

Some reaps use the hips as well as the legs. One example of this is the hip sweep, or *hara goshi*.

The Hip Sweep

In the hip sweep, attackers lift their right leg as they turn to the left. This sweeps their opponent off their feet.

The Large Inner Reap

Speed is crucial in the two-handed reap. If it is not done quickly, the opponent can twist away from the attack.

1 *Start the attack with your feet shoulder-width apart and your right foot slightly forwards. Grip the opponent's collar and sleeve.*

2 *Step forward and put your right leg in between your opponent's legs. Push forwards with your right hand, and pull on the opponent's sleeve. Hook your right leg behind your opponent's left leg. Sweep it back towards you, keeping your foot sliding along the ground. Carry on pushing with your right hand. Bring your left leg in, and sweep the opponent's left leg out to the side and away.*

Large and Small Reaps

A 'large' reap is one where the attacker uses their leg to sweep the opponent off their feet. In a 'small' reap, the attacker uses their foot instead.

Reaps Using Hands

In some reaps, *judoka* use their hands. In the two-handed reap, for example, the attacker grabs the back of the opponent's legs. Next the attacker pushes their shoulder into the opponent's belt and throws

This type of attack is very popular with *judoka* who follow a 'wrestling' style. These *judoka* often come from countries where wrestling is a popular activity. Many of these countries were once part of the USSR (the Union of Soviet Socialist Republics – see page 29).

Groundwork

Of course, when you manage to throw someone using judo, the fight may not be over. It may have to carry on, on the ground. When the fight carries on in this way, it is called groundwork.

Hold-downs

Hold-downs are just what they sound like – ways of holding someone down on the ground. In competition, it is possible to win by holding your opponent down for 25 seconds. In self-defence, being able to hold someone down until they give up is a very useful skill.

Contest Groundwork

In a contest, the judges call out "*Osaekomi!*" (the Japanese word for hold-down) when they think a hold-down has begun. The judges only call *osaekomi* if they think these four things have all happened:

1) The attacker is in the correct position.
2) The defender is being controlled by the attacker, and has at least one shoulder and their back on the mat.
3) The attacker's legs are free of the defender.
4) At least one *judoka* has part of their body inside the contest area.

Once the judges call *osaekomi*, the countdown begins. If the defender has not got free within 25 seconds, the attacker wins.

This is the scarf hold, which in Japanese is *kesa gatame*. It is one of the first groundwork holds new *judoka* learn. Wrap your right arm around your opponent's neck (like a scarf). Hold on to their left arm and pin it across your body. Use your bodyweight to pin your opponent down.

Bridging is one of the best ways to escape a hold-down during a contest.

Defending Against Hold-downs

There are two main ways of escaping from a hold-down in a competition. They are armlocks and bridging.

Bridging is making a bridge shape with your body, by lifting your hips off the mat. Sometimes bridging forces the attacker to roll off. In contests, bridging at least stops the defender's back from touching the floor. This means that the countdown stops, and has to start at the beginning when their back touches the floor.

Armlocks are used by top *judoka* to fight against a hold-down. Armlocks put pressure on the attacker's elbow joint. The defender aims to force the attacker to let go, or give up the fight completely.

In contests, at least one *judoka* must have part of their body inside the contest area (red in this photograph) during a hold-down – even if it is only a little part!

25

In Competition

Judoka *enter contests as a way of showing they have made progress. Contests also help them move up the grades, to a higher belt colour.*

Contests and How They Work

Judo contests are knockout competitions similar to tennis tournaments. If you win your first bout, you go through to the next round. If you win that one, you go through again. If you keep winning contests, you end up in the final, fighting the only other person who has won all their fights.

Contest Points Scoring

The scoring system used in judo contests is based on the techniques that each *judoka* demonstrates to the judges. In order (highest score first) these are:

1) *Ippon* – this score wins the contest. It is awarded for:
   • throwing the opponent on their back with force
   • submission by the opponent
   • a 25-second hold-down.

2) *Waza-ari* – this score beats all other lower scores, however many of the lower scores the opponent has been given. It is awarded for:
   • Throwing the opponent with force but partly on their side.
   • A 21–25-second hold-down.

3) *Yuko* – one *yuko* beats any number of lower scores. It is awarded for:
   • Throwing your opponent without force on to their side or back
   • a 16–20-second hold-down.

David Douillet is one of the most successful *judoka* ever. He is a national hero in France, where he has inspired many young people to take up judo.

David Douillet

Date of birth: February 17, 1969

Nationality: French

Contest record:

• Olympic gold medalist 1996, 2000

• World champion 1993, 1995, 1997

Soon after winning Olympic gold in 1996, David Douillet was involved in a serious motorbike accident. He recovered to win the world championship in 1997, then his second Olympic gold medal in 2000.

4) *Koka* – this score is awarded for:
   • Throwing your opponent on to their thigh or bottom
   • a 10–15-second hold-down.

Types of Contest

There are lots of different types of contest. Young *judoka* can enter inter-club contests, for example. Or they can enter mini-*mon* contests, which are only open to players of a lower grade.

Top-level *judoka* can enter regional tournaments like the European Championships or Asian Games. There are also international one-off contests called 'Super A' tournaments.

The aim of every top *judoka* is to win at the World Championships and the Olympic Games. The best fighters in the world are at these contests, and winning them takes a huge amount of hard work.

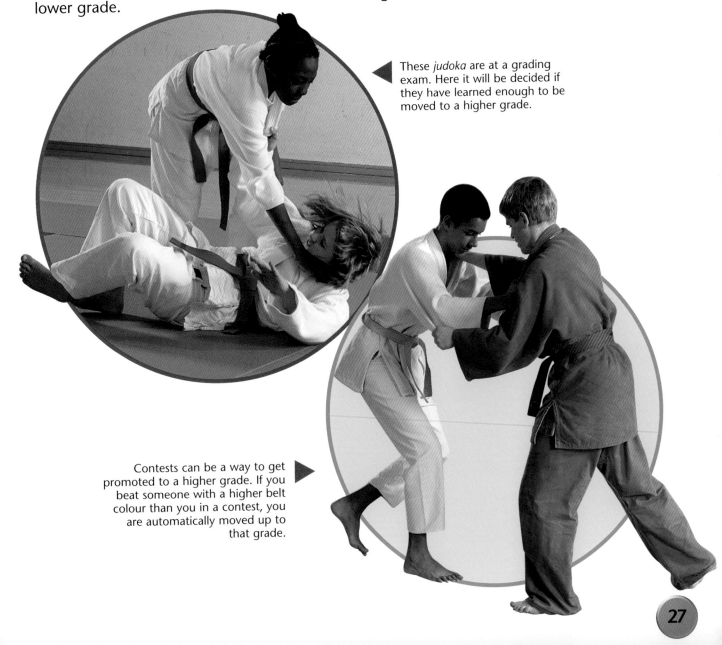

◀ These *judoka* are at a grading exam. Here it will be decided if they have learned enough to be moved to a higher grade.

Contests can be a way to get promoted to a higher grade. If you beat someone with a higher belt colour than you in a contest, you are automatically moved up to that grade. ▶

World and Olympic Champions

Men's Judo Champions

Weight category	2004 Olympic Champion	2005 World Champion
Open	–	Midori Shintani, Japan
Over 100kg	Keiji Suzuki, Japan	Dennis van der Geest, NL
Below 100kg	Ihar Makarau, Belarus	Aleksandr Mikhailine, Russia
Below 90kg	Zurab Zviadauri, Georgia	Keiji Suzuki, Japan
Below 81kg	Ilias Iliadis, Greece	Hiroshi Izumi, Japan
Below 73kg	Won Hee Lee, S. Korea	Guillaume Elmont, NL
Below 66kg	Masato Uchishiba, Japan	Akos Braun, Hungary
Below 60kg	Tadahiro Nomura, Japan	JD Junior, Brazil
		Craig Fallon, Britain

Women's Judo Champions

Weight category	2004 Olympic Champion	2005 World Champion
Open	–	Midori Shintani, Japan
Over 78kg	Maki Tsukada, Japan	Wen Tong, China
Below 78kg	Noriko Anno, Japan	Yurisel Laborde, Cuba
Below 70kg	Masae Ueno, Japan	Edith Bosch, NL
Below 63kg	Ayumi Tanimoto, Japan	Lucie Decosse, France
Below 57kg	Yvonne Boenisch, Germany	Sun Hui Kye, N. Korea
Below 52kg	Dongmei Xian, China	Ying Li, China
Below 48kg	Ryoko Tamura, Japan	Yanet Bermoy, Cuba

*There is no Open category in the Olympics, where fighters are only allowed to compete in their own weight division.

The three most successful competition judoka 1951-2001

1= Ingrid Berghmans (Belgium): 6 world, 1 Olympic titles
1= Ryoko Tamura (Japan): 6 world, 1 Olympic titles
3 David Douillet (France): 4 world, 2 Olympic titles

Glossary

Aggression Attacking or threatening behaviour.

Bout Another name for a judo match; a contest between two *judoka*.

Discipline Obedience and determination, especially in training.

Dojo A place where judo is practised. The place may be used only for judo, or it may be shared with other activities.

Gi The special clothes that *judoka* wear for practice or contests.

Groundwork The name for the continuation of a judo contest once the *judoka* are no longer standing up.

Hara goshi A hip-sweep throw.

Judoka A person who takes part in judo.

Kesa gatame A basic groundwork technique, whose name means 'scarf hold'. It is used to pin your opponent to the floor.

Kumikata When a *judoka* grabs hold of their opponent.

Kuzushi The art of breaking an opponent's balance, making it possible to throw them.

Kyu A judo grade for senior, older *judoka*.

Leverage points Particular spots where a push or pull helps you to move an object.

Mon A junior judo grade, for younger *judoka*.

Morote seoi nage A two-handed shoulder throw.

Ogoshi The large hip throw.

Reaping throws Throws that sweep an opponent off their feet.

Respect Determination to treat people well, with honour and consideration.

Tatami The area used for judo practice and contests.

Technique A way of carrying out a physical action as well as possible.

Ukemi 'Breakfalls', which are ways to make a fall less forceful.

Uki goshi A floating hip throw.

USSR A country that no longer exists. The USSR was governed from Russia, but included large areas of Asia as well.

Websites

www.ijf.org
The website of the International Judo Federation, which organizes the world championships and Olympic contests. This site also provides links to various regional organizations such as European judo's governing body.

www.twoj.org
The website for the official magazine of the British Judo Federation.

www.judoinfo.com
As the name suggests, this site is useful for all sorts of judo-related information, including the history of judo, techniques, training and – best of all – a section of (mostly terrible) judo jokes.

www.judoaustralia.com.au
This site has links to many other judo-related sites, both Australian and international.

Note to parents and teachers: every effort has been made by the Publishers to ensure that these websites are suitable for children, that they are of the highest educational value, and that they contain no inappropriate or offensive material. However, because of the nature of the Internet, it is impossible to guarantee that the contents of these sites will not be altered. We strongly advise that Internet access is supervised by a responsible adult.

Index